Contents

About the authors

Mayor Frank Branston

Frank Branston became Bedford's first directly elected mayor in October 2002. His current term of office ends in May 2007 when he would be eligible for re-election. Prior to becoming Mayor, Frank had been a journalist for most of his working life.

Mayor Steve Bullock

Steve Bullock became Lewisham's first directly elected mayor in May 2002, having previously been leader of the council during the late 1990s. He has had a twin track career in local government and the NHS, and immediately prior to his election was serving a second term as chair of University Hospital Lewisham.

Mayor Stuart Drummond

Stuart Drummond became Hartlepool's first directly elected mayor in May 2002 and was re-elected in 2005 with a vastly increased majority of over 10,000. He is Chair of the Safer Hartlepool Partnership and Vice-Chair of the Hartlepool Partnership.

Mayor Mark Meredith

Mark Meredith became Stoke-on-Trent's second directly elected mayor in May 2005. The first Labour Mayor in the city - his predecessor having been an independent. Mark was born and educated in the area and celebrated his 40th birthday while in office. As a local business man and political activist, Mark has the interests of the City at heart.

Mayor Dorothy Thornhill

Dorothy Thornhill became Watford's first directly elected mayor in May 2002. She is the only Liberal Democrat mayor, and was the first woman to be elected to such a post. Dorothy previously worked for twenty-five years as a teacher.

Mayor Robin Wales

Mayor Robin Wales became Newham's first directly elected mayor in May 2002, having been leader of Newham Council since 1995. Sir Robin was awarded a knighthood in 2000 in recognition of his services to local government.

Mayor Martin Winter

Martin Winter became Doncaster's first directly elected mayor in May 2002 and was re-elected in May 2005. Prior to becoming mayor, Martin was for a number of years the National Training Development Manager for the Royal Society for Nature Conservation.

Kiran Dhillon

Kiran Dhillon joined the New Local Government Network in July 2004, having previously worked for two years in a London local authority. Kiran runs NLGN's Mayoral Forum, which seeks to understand and disseminate the lessons of directly elected mayors in practice. She also runs NLGN's local authority Innovation Network, studying local government innovation and linking councils' experiences at the frontline to national policy debates. Kiran is co-author of the NLGN report *Making Community Leadership Real* (with Anna Randle, NLGN 2005).

Acknowledgements

I am grateful to all of the authors of the essays that follow for their intellectual contribution to the ongoing debate about elected mayors; and also to those other members of our Mayoral Forum who have on this occasion not contributed.

I also wish to thank former and current colleagues at the New Local Government Network for their support and advice throughout the course of this work, in particular Ian Parker, Anna Randle and Dick Sorabji.

Kiran Dhillon
March 2006

Foreword

Mayor Mark Meredith

As a newly elected Mayor I am delighted that the New Local Government Network has asked me to write the foreword for this exciting new publication.

Stoke-on-Trent is in a unique position as the only local authority in the UK with the Council Manager/elected mayor system of governance. This has proved to be very unpopular with councillors who feel completely excluded from the decision-making processes. A referendum has been promised in 2007 and it may well be that a change in management arrangements will follow. Whatever system is chosen however, no changes will be effective until 2009.

My life has not been made easy by the fact that 59 of the 60 Councillors are fundamentally opposed to the model of management in the City. Outside of the Council there is a considerable confusion between the role of the Lord Mayor (i.e. the Civic Head of the Council) and the elected Mayor. I am regularly asked where my car and chain of office has been left. Protocol is also very sensitive, making sure that I take my "rightful" place in the Civic Hierarchy is vital given the number of people I would offend by getting it wrong! There is also a serious issue about resources for a mayoral office. Staffing and modern equipment remain an issue and an almost continuous battle.

Just over six months in to my new role, I am starting to see the possibilities and limitations of the position. The Budget process for the forthcoming year has certainly thrown up some difficulties; whereas at the same time, I can see real benefits from properly targeted regeneration in the city. I am not convinced that I was initially prepared for everything that was thrown at me. Finding a proper work/life balance is also difficult and I am having to learn to say "no" more often.

Mayors elsewhere have been incredibly successful. Earlier research suggested that in most mayoral authorities, most people knew they had an elected mayor, knew their name and clearly identified the Mayor as the person who ran the local council. With further evidence emerging that this is true (see Steve Bullock's essay in this collection), this is one of the clearest benefits of the system – one individual is held accountable in the eyes of the electorate for the decisions which most affect their lives.

Partner organisations also welcome the mayoral position and this has been very much the case in Stoke-on-Trent. Regeneration has been extremely successful over the last few months. With a Mayor promoting the city and bringing the agencies together, considerable funds and expertise has been brought in.

This is an exciting time for local government, there are many changes posed for all elected politicians but elected mayors are in the vanguard of these. The Local Government White Paper due to be published later this year will, I hope, define more clearly the powers and role of elected mayors.

For the Mayoral model adopted by Stoke-on-Trent to be successful there needs to be a good relationship between the Mayor and Council Manager – based on honesty, trust and a commitment from both, to the delivery of excellent services. The relationship is however, not one of equals – ultimately, the Council Manager makes the decisions and the Mayor gives political and policy advice. It is a democratic deficit which must be addressed.

My belief is that mayoral systems, in whatever form are here to stay – it is up to the office holders to ensure that they make the best of the benefits for their electorate.

1 Introduction: elected mayors – the direction of travel

Kiran Dhillon

For almost a decade, the idea of directly elected mayors has been much debated across local government in England. Enthusiasts of the mayoral system, optimistic that the idea of mayors would take off, have consistently argued that it can revive local democracy through strengthened leadership, accountability, public engagement and quicker decision-making.

In 2004, two years after the first handful of local authority mayors were elected, NLGN published a report evaluating the early lessons. In doing so, we helped move the debate beyond the earlier ideological stand-off to an evidence-based assessment of what the mayoral model – as opposed to individual mayors – had delivered up to that point. The report, which received widespread attention, concluded that the mayoral model was progressing well.[1]

Polling carried out in 2003 (and referred to in the NLGN report) revealed that on average, elected mayors were at that point known to 57% of local people – over double the percentage of a council leader. In the North East, where three of the original mayors were elected, this figure rose to 73% and was still 26% in London where the three borough mayors were struggling with weak local media and some confusion with the Mayor of London.

While it was too early to judge the long-term impact of mayors on service delivery, the services on which they had focussed – particularly liveability and street scene – had improved. No mayoral council had slid down the Comprehensive Performance Assessment table, in fact several climbed up. There were also signs that elected mayors were offering a new form of community leadership. Mayors described themselves as 'mayor of the town' rather than of the council, and sought to influence agendas beyond the direct remit of the authority. Many of the mayors sought a consensual approach, seeking to engage with local agencies.

---

1 Randle, A. (2004) *Mayors Mid-term: Lessons from the first eighteen months of directly elected mayors*, London: New Local Government Network

In short, the NLGN report concluded that there were many areas where mayors were making a difference: services were improving; there were high levels of recognition amongst local citizens and mayors were developing new relationships with local partners.

At around the same time, NLGN also published a collection of essays on the governance of London, in which many of the contributors welcomed the emergence of a Mayor for London.[2] The mayor was seen as providing a focus for key stakeholders in the capital; as well as a general feeling that the position gave London a strong figurehead, advocate and ambassador, who strengthened its ability to compete with major cities around the world. In terms of profile meanwhile, a team from MORI writing in the collection, noted how Ken Livingstone had an 81% recognition rating among Londoners as the Mayor.[3]

While it is true that there are currently only thirteen elected mayors (Livingstone plus a dozen local authority mayors), they are very much part of the new political landscape in England. More importantly however, there is now a fresh political impetus to explore their potential. Supportive comments have been voiced by the new leader of the Conservative Party, David Cameron.[4] Meanwhile, in its 2005 General Election manifesto the Labour Party offered the following promise:

'We will explore giving people a more direct opportunity to express a view about whether they would like to have a directly elected mayor. We will also consult with city councils on the powers needed for a new generation of city mayors'.[5]

The debate about elected mayors also feeds into wider debates about local governance. Whether considering neighbourhoods, unitarisation or leadership, we are ultimately trying to answer a question about what we want our local governance system to deliver.

The fundamental principle underpinning these discussions is that our local governance system should deliver strong, accountable, visible and responsive leadership. It should be capable of delivering improvements in our localities by

2 Corry, D. (ed) (2004) *London Calling: reflections on four years of the GLA and solutions for the future,* London: New Local Government Network

3 Colling, A., Kaur-Ballagan, K. and Fraser, P. (2004) 'The People of London' in Corry, D. (ed) op.cit.

4 See for example, news coverage of speech by Rt Hon David Cameron MP to Crime Concern audience *The Guardian,* 16 January 2006

5 The Labour Party (2005) *The Labour Party Manifesto 2005,* London: The Labour Party

offering a vision for the area. In doing so, it should be pulling local partners together to deliver joined-up services, attracting inward investment and driving economic development, and listening to the demands of citizens. We are therefore, looking for a governance system capable of delivering excellent services and re-engaging people with political institutions.

Any form of organising local democracy will carry certain benefits and drawbacks, opportunities and risks. And so we must be aware of the question we are seeking to answer when considering local government reform. This then allows us to weigh up the relative benefits and drawbacks of each approach. Directly elected mayors can provide one piece of the local governance jigsaw. Last year's 'local:vision' document on the future of local leadership, published by the Office of the Deputy Prime Minister identified their potential:

'Mayors can provide a focus for public engagement and bringing partners together. The fact that mayors have the unique mandate of being a single individual elected by citizens from across the locality as a whole reinforces their legitimacy and can enhance their ability to act as a leader of the entire community, to bring partners together and to shape services and outcomes well beyond the immediate responsibilities of the council.'[6]

While it is too early to draw definite conclusions, the current collection of essays revisits some of the debates about the possibilities of the mayoral system and – with the benefit of the experiences of the early pioneers – illustrates what it is capable of delivering. As a form of political leadership what merits and advantages does it have over the council leader/cabinet model? And what can we learn from the mayoral system that can inform broader debates about local government reform?

The essays that follow give a number of the current crop of elected mayors a chance to offer their views on how mayoral governance has had a real impact on their local areas. The authors cover a range of areas, focusing on some key features of the mayoral system, including public engagement, and the ability to attract inward investment and promote economic development.

Watford mayor Dorothy Thornhill discusses how despite her initial opposition to the idea of directly elected mayors, she now believes they are a route to

---

6 Office of the Deputy Prime Minister (2005) *Vibrant Local Leadership*, London: ODPM, p.14

enhancing local democracy, through their visibility and accountability. Hartlepool mayor Stuart Drummond agrees with this assertion and believes that mayors are high profile community leaders, capable of connecting the public with local government. Meanwhile, Lewisham mayor Steve Bullock discusses how mayoral governance has provided him with opportunities to reach out to the public and local partners.

As well as delivering responsive and visible leadership, mayoral governance can also deliver tangible improvements in localities. Bedford mayor Frank Branston describes how he has set about regenerating his borough, while Doncaster mayor Martin Winter discusses his success in the area of economic development. Finally, Newham mayor Robin Wales focuses on how mayoral governance has been key to tackling local problems of anti-social behaviour.

In the round, the authors reveal that there are definite benefits to the mayoral system. The current incumbents – including those not contributing to this collection – are seizing the community leadership role; providing a vision for the area; representing and acting as ambassadors for their localities; attracting investment; using their mandate to bring local partners together; and providing a clear focus for citizen engagement. In doing so, they not only enhance local democracy but ensure better and more responsive services for local residents.

The question for NLGN and others, therefore, is what can we learn from actual existing mayoral governance in the UK? The experience of the local authority mayors and that of Ken Livingstone in London, does offer some food for thought about the future of the model and the scope for city mayors, or indeed city region mayors. It also allows us to consider how these lessons might be applicable to a system of directly elected cabinets? Reflections on some of these questions are given in the concluding chapter.

2 *Directly elected mayors: making local government more accountable*

Mayor Dorothy Thornhill

When the 2001 Local Government Act was passed, some people hoped that directly elected mayors would be the big idea to revive local democracy. As many from the first batch of mayors reach the end of their terms, it is clear that this has not happened.

The political parties quickly lost enthusiasm for the idea once it appeared that the main beneficiaries of mayoral elections were Independent candidates with no previous involvement in politics. Local councillors also regard the concept with some suspicion because more power for elected mayors can mean less for other elected members. So the bandwagon has resolutely failed to roll. In particular, the big cities, which one might have expected to be keenest to opt for an elected mayor, have stayed aloof.

For the past four years I have served as elected mayor of Watford, a small district council, outside London but within the M25. The electorate will of course get their chance to return their verdict on my performance through the ballot box, but I believe that the system of having an elected mayor has been a success and that they help to create effective and accountable local government. In this I am departing from the orthodoxy of my own party, the Liberal Democrats, who are strong localists but against the idea of elected mayors.

Given that I originally opposed the idea of elected mayors, I am more than aware that there are disadvantages of the system. Britain has a tradition of parliamentary democracy, rather than direct election of the executive. This means that the elected representatives who see the executive operating day-to-day, whether councillors or MPs, hold it to account on behalf of the electorate. Many councillors feel that their ability to do this is reduced under a mayoral system. They feel their mandate is diminished. Under the cabinet system, councillors as a whole are no longer responsible for many decisions. With elected mayors, councillors do not even get to choose the executive of their council. It also requires a two-thirds majority to overturn a mayoral policy or proposal, even in those areas that remain in the discretion of full council.

Fortunately, I have had a simple majority for all the proposals I have put to full council in the last four years and have not had to invoke the two-thirds rule. But I can imagine the frustration that councillors would feel if the wishes of a majority in the council chamber were regularly over-ridden by a mayor. I can imagine that had I lost the election in 2002, four more years languishing in opposition have given me a rather different perspective on elected mayors.

I have however, come to the conclusion that the strengths of elected mayors in enhancing our local democracy outweigh the drawbacks. The first positive thing I noticed about the mayoral system related to the election itself. One of the problems of local democracy in Britain is the way in which elections, which are supposedly about the delivery of local services, become a verdict on the popularity of the national government. Where local factors do make a difference, very often this is at the level of the very local – concerning neighbourhood issues or how hard local councillors work in their wards. This creates a local democratic deficit in that local elections take place without campaigns properly addressing the most important question of who has the best policies to run the local authority. This can be corrected by a direct mayoral election. Candidates have to talk about how they will run the council, what their priorities are and what policies they will pursue. In Watford we even saw the return of hustings debates between the candidates – something that had not happened in a local election for decades. So the mayoral elections themselves can help to make local government more accountable.

Secondly, it is true that with an elected mayor people do know who to praise or blame for the success or failure of the council. Local government can be very anonymous. Perhaps in large cities where evening newspapers give extensive coverage to local politics, citizens will know the names of the council leader and the main cabinet members. But often it can be unclear to the average citizen who is responsible for decisions. A move to cabinet government has not solved that. In Watford, people know who the mayor is and expect to be able to raise issues with me about the way the council is run. My office gets upwards of 150 contacts each week on a range of subjects from local residents, a level of contact that was unknown when there was a council leader.

What is heartening is that residents feel that there is someone in the town hall whose job it is to be on their side and who can make a difference to the issues that are concerning them. Residents are saying: 'We elected you and we expect you to be able to account for the way the council is run'. It is a step forward for local democracy if people know who is the political head of their local authority and feel able to contact them in the knowledge that they won't pass the buck. Politicians are often accused of being shameless self-publicists – always making a dash to get in front of the cameras or a quote in the paper. But of course it is an essential part of a functioning democracy that people know who represents them. In this sense too, the elected mayor system has enhanced our local democracy.

Thirdly, elected mayors have an implicit remit that goes wider than the affairs of their local authority. We talk about someone being leader of a council but mayor of a town or city. There is an expectation that the mayor's role is not just about making sure that the council's services are well run, but will extend to having a clear vision for the future of their town or city and to bringing together other public and private agencies to achieve that vision. One of my proudest achievements as elected mayor of Watford was in helping to bring together a range of public and private sector bodies to get agreement for a new hospital and health campus in the town. While I am not saying that a council leader could not have done this, having the direct mandate from the electorate of Watford certainly enhanced the moral authority I could carry in getting agreement for the project.

This brings me to the fourth point – elected mayors help to enhance the status of local government and overcome the sense that it is the 'Cinderella' of British democracy. This is partly due to the simple fact that being an elected mayor is clearly a full-time job, seen as being on a par with a member of parliament. With the exception of Ken Livingstone, there are no local government figures whose names could even remotely be described as household words. Journalists on national newspapers who cover politics seem bored by local government. Westminster is where it's at, the home of the big beasts. Town halls are tiresome and dull. Even in a party as committed to local government as the Liberal Democrats, the political anoraks who can name all the party's MPs would probably not even be able to name half of its council leaders.

This may seem a rather frivolous point, but democracy depends on an informed electorate who are able to engage with the issues. There is extensive television and newspaper coverage of national politics, but relatively little of local government. I believe that, having been chosen by an electorate of similar size to, or in some cases much bigger than, members of parliament, elected mayors could have the credibility to put local government back on the wider political map.

Far more fundamental than how the political heads of local authorities are elected, a more serious problem is the continued low esteem in which local government is held within our political system. Although all three major parties are now talking about localism, we need to see real evidence of the willingness of the centre to let go. It needs a change in our whole political culture. Recently, I watched on television a panel discussion of leading political journalists about Tony Blair's 'respect' agenda. What was remarkable is that although the panellists covered different shades of the political spectrum, all seemed to agree that reliance on action by local authorities was a weakness of the Prime Minister's initiative. There was not a hint that it might actually be positive that local authorities should have the ability to identify their own local priorities rather than slavishly following those of central government. Local government has much to do to reassert its credibility.

There are no final right or wrong answers to how we organise our democracy. My own political party is firmly in favour of localism but against elected mayors. Yet on the continent and in America, local government is more highly valued than in Britain and they elect their mayors directly. Over the last four years I have with some reluctance come to the conclusion that any dangers of a mayoral system are outweighed by the greater accountability to the electorate, the increased recognition of who is responsible for decision-making and the increased credibility for local government that comes with elected mayors.

3 *Elected mayors as true community leaders*

Mayor Stuart Drummond

The mayoral system is working! There are plenty of people who might say differently but the results speak for themselves. The system has certainly delivered in Hartlepool and, looking around at the other eleven mayoral authorities, those areas certainly seem to be going from strength to strength as well.

My perception of what the mayoral system should achieve is, among other things, greater accountability for decision-making, higher profile community leadership and increased public involvement in local government. If this perception is accurate, then it will not be long until elected mayors are back at the top of the Government's agenda and appearing all over the country.

I have been elected by the public of Hartlepool and entrusted by them to lead the town forward and take the difficult decisions along the way. I believe people appreciate this and the huge majority of townsfolk are willing to help and support me in my efforts to make Hartlepool a better place to live. Being an Independent has helped me greatly. The political history of the town does not make very good reading and I think people were sick of the back biting and squabbling of the main political parties. They saw that having an elected mayor was a fresh opportunity to take the town forward and make a new start.

Of course there was a lot of scepticism and caution at first, especially considering the circumstances in which I was elected. A lot has been written about why I upset the apple cart. There were a variety of reasons for my election the first time around, but my re-election was certainly no fluke. I increased my majority from just over 600 to well over 10,200. This was great for me, but just as importantly, a fantastic boost for the elected mayoral system.

I think trust played a huge part in my re-election. There is a perception that politicians can't be trusted, quite often because they make promises they can't and don't deliver. I have been honest from day one and tried not to hide anything from the public. I made no secret that I was on a very steep learning curve and if there was something I didn't know, I would say so. I think people appreciated that.

I believe the main reason I was so convincingly re-elected was that I delivered on my promises. Probably my most successful initiative to date has been 'Operation Cleansweep'. I have pulled together many partner agencies including the police, fire brigade, health, Jobcentre Plus, probation and of course the Council's departments. We go into an area of the town each month for around a week and blitz it. There are between fifty and eighty highly visible people, out on the streets cleaning up the place, removing graffiti, fly-tipping and litter. There are home fire safety visits, extra police patrols, the removal of untaxed cars, and the repairing of street furniture and the roads. And it all costs virtually nothing.

This has been going for over two years now and we have covered over two thirds of the town. It is very high impact and we have found that people are so impressed that they continue to take pride and ownership of their own area after we have left. In fact, three or four resident's groups have been set up on the back of Cleansweep. The scheme has had national recognition as best practice and many other local authorities are now taking on similar schemes.

This is an initiative that, as Mayor, I can put into action without having to clear it through any party or formal decision-making process. I simply used my influence to run a good idea past people at the top of the various organisations, and we went with it. It is a huge advantage of the mayoral system that I can do this and it gives me great opportunities to try out new ideas.

I saw one of my first roles as mayor to reconnect Hartlepool Borough Council back to the public and vice versa. In the past, most decisions were taken behind closed doors and the public did not really know who was doing what. Those days are long gone. The public now know exactly where to come if they need a problem sorting or if they want to blame someone for something not to their liking. The buck well and truly stops with me. If someone gets in touch with me with an issue, I will contact them personally – no matter how big or small the problem – and try and deal with it or at least point them in the right direction. I see this part of my job as being a type of 'super-councillor'.

As Mayor, I have been very keen to engage with the public. Not only do I try to meet people in the town, but I also actively encourage people to become involved in decision-making. All of our council, cabinet and portfolio meetings are open for members of the public to come along to and ask questions, which they quite often do. I have taken a handful of cabinet meetings out into the community and one of the most enjoyable and successful meetings we had was held in a local secondary school with pupils taking part in a junior 'Question Time'. Each year, I hold a 'State of the Borough' debate at which members of the public get an hour to question me on any subject.

Hartlepool has three neighbourhood forums on which elected resident representatives sit. We also have over 100 resident groups or committees and an incredibly strong voluntary sector with whom we engage. I often call Hartlepool the biggest village in the country. Although we have a population of around 90,000, everyone seems to know everyone else and I would be shocked if anywhere in Britain had a stronger community spirit than Hartlepool. It is my role to capture this enthusiasm from the community and help to channel it in the same direction as the other partners who are working towards the same goals.

All of the elected mayors are seen as community leaders across the full town or borough rather than just the local council. There is an expectation from the public that I should deal with issues affecting health trusts, policing, further education and so on. I am fortunate that partnership working is strong in Hartlepool and working relationships are very good, so it is quite easy for me, at the moment, to speak to other leaders in local organisations to try and get things done.

I feel that the leaders in other local organisations will come to me because I am the Mayor. They see it as a way of getting things done. It encourages me that these people do come to me frequently and seem to be working in the spirit of true partnership. I have a good relationship with our business community. It is encouraging that business leaders in the town see the Mayor as having the influence and leadership to help the local economy.

The mayoral governance model is still very much in its early days and undoubtedly there are ways in which it can be improved. There is now an excellent opportunity for the Government to look at the mayoral model and implement some improvements that will see elected mayors given real responsibility over other public bodies. Local Area Agreements could be the vehicles to do this. The regionalisation agenda seems to be ploughing ahead in the North East despite the resounding 'No' vote from the public just over a year ago. The police, fire service, Primary Care Trust, the Learning and Skills Council, and Connexions all seem to be going or are under the threat of going regional. If the Council could govern and commission these services, decision-making would be kept at a local level and the elected mayor would be even more accountable for the public services on his or her patch.

There is stability with an elected mayor. Most of us have a four year term of office. We can plan ahead over a much longer period than a council leader, who worries about reselection each year. We can get on and work towards a long term strategy knowing that we will be there a few years down the line, and therefore a step on the way along the road to achieving our aims. During this time we can gather support from all areas without partners fearing that they have to start from square one each year and build new relationships. It really does give everyone clarity.

I seem to remember that, a little over four years ago, the Government sold the ideas of elected mayors based on the American model. In practice an elected mayor in England has a fraction of the responsibility of their American counterpart. The Government now has the opportunity to give elected mayors a greater remit. If they aspire to have true community leaders, they must act now.

4 *Leadership through consensus building*

Mayor Steve Bullock

It's 2:00am on the first day of a new year on a damp, apparently deserted street in South London. Suddenly a hooded figure steps out of the shadows and moves towards me. As I mentally debate whether to be conciliatory or belligerent, a hand is thrust towards me. The figure says "Happy New Year Mr Mayor – I met you when you came to our school…"

Mayoral governance was intended to facilitate two things – leadership and transparency. As our young student demonstrated, transparency has been achieved. People in Lewisham know I am their mayor and through the ballot box they will give their judgement on the success or failure of my efforts on their behalf.

But what evidence will they base that judgement upon? What did we set out to achieve, how did we do it and did having an elected mayor make a difference?

Following my election in May 2002 I set out to win the confidence and support of a range of individuals and organisations, not only for my decision-making to be better informed but also because delivering change and improvement requires the active efforts of those same individuals and organisations. In other words the focus of my mayoralty was intended to be leadership, but a leadership based on consensus building.

Prior to my election I attempted to set out what I would seek to do as mayor. Among other things I pledged to:

- be open, be accessible and work in consultation with the people and the diverse communities of our borough on the major issues which affect all our lives; and

- lead a partnership between the Council, community, private sector and other public services to improve the economic, social and environmental well-being of the borough.

I want to now look at how we have tried to do this, and the extent to which we have succeeded.

Being open and accessible

There have been three strands to building an open and accessible mayoralty in Lewisham. Mayoral visits to community organisations, media work and a major consultation programme 'Lewisham Listens'.

Personal contact with people is the most effective form of communications. But it is also a challenge when you are serving a population of a quarter of a million souls, and mayoral visits play a crucial role. These have developed from the many invitations 'Civic' mayors receive. I have consciously tried to accept invitations that fit within a strategy to reach out across the borough to all sections of the community. At one extreme there is the annual pensioners' conference attended by over 600 active and vocal local citizens. But at the other extreme, meetings with a handful of residents who have a shared concern are just as much part of the dialogue. The result has been that I have met people and visited places as Mayor which I never reached in five years as council leader.

These 'civic' events and meetings have been complemented by a programme of day long visits to each of Lewisham's electoral wards. The visits involved meeting as many community groups and local service providers and users as possible. Each visit culminated in an open meeting at which the local community were able to raise any issues of concern with council officials. I deliberately took on the role of host and advocate for the community at these meetings, letting officers explain the services they run on behalf of the community. This advocacy approach has been fundamental to engaging with communities. It enables people to work with me to explore options rather than create a 'them and us' barrier between me as Mayor and the community.

The second element of my approach has been to reach out via the local press and media. Of course local newspapers still run negative stories. Falling numbers of staff and increased competition leave little time for journalists to grasp complex issues, let alone explain them to the public. Simplistic headlines are also more likely to sell papers.

My strategy has therefore been based on being personally open with local journalists and willing to provide comment, quotes and information when requested. A sense of proportion and a steely determination are prerequisites of a successful strategy. This has been backed up by the authority adapting its communications to the mayoralty. As Mayor I am the primary council spokesperson on our corporate priority issues. A proactive media approach, making news not just responding to it, has helped ensure that the public know what I and the Council are trying to do. Using our own communications, such as our civic magazine, has also allowed us to engage directly with people. We have returned again and again to issues such as graffiti, recycling and community safety. The message does eventually get across.

Consultation is the third element of my approach. Only when people can see that their views are listened to, do they feel they will actively engage in dialogue. I have introduced a mayoral consultation board. This oversees all council consultations from individual street works surveys to the annual residents survey. This ensures that it is conducted in a meaningful way, without duplication and that it is properly evaluated. To give the public confidence in consultation I have also ensured that the Council provides proper feedback. The results, including what we have changed as a result of consultation, are regularly reported to residents via our council magazine and website.

The evidence from our most recent residents' survey indicates that community engagement, effective media management and meaningful consultation are working. Seven out of ten residents think we are doing a good job, that the Council is well run and that we keep people informed. Recognition of the Mayor is at an all time high – at 38% in November 2005, compared to 16% two years previously.

Citizens also believe we are doing what we say we are doing. 66% of Lewisham residents agree that the Council cares for the environment and 48% believe that the Council and our partners are reducing crime and anti-social behaviour.

69% of Lewisham's residents think the Council is doing a good job – the third consecutive year this figure has increased and one which is now 5% above the London average.

It may be hard work but engaging with people directly, through the local press and real consultation works. It builds trust and support from the community and it proves to partners that I really can speak on behalf of all the residents of my borough.

Improving public services through partnership

The notion of partnership working is one that has been around in Lewisham for many years and there was already a good level of cooperation between public agencies and others. My pledge should be seen as working with the grain locally but seeking to take things to a new level. The Lewisham Local Strategic Partnership (LSP) was already in existence but at a very early stage in its development. An early decision by the LSP was that the Mayor should chair it. This was taken in the knowledge that Lewisham was about to embark on a different form of local governance, and that whoever was Mayor would have a wider role than had previously been ascribed to council leaders.

The relationship between the LSP and the Council is a good one, relatively devoid of suspicions and power struggles. The organisation has begun to mature and increasingly adopt a shared perspective rather than arguing for particular sectors. There is an inevitable tension between the aspiration for LSPs to be driving an agenda which raises achievement and attainment in local communities and the role of the local authority in providing community leadership. LSPs do not deliver services themselves but act through others. The Council, as the largest service provider, as well as the one with the widest range of service responsibilities, must be a key player.

I have sought to reconcile the two roles of the Council, democratic and service provision, through the opportunities provided by our governance arrangements. In my role as chair I am supported and advised by a small team located in the Mayor's office reporting to a senior officer also located there. This gives me the freedom to act independently of the Council's role as a service provider. Some cabinet members with responsibilities for relevant service areas also sit on the LSP but they are advised by the executive directors through a quite separate reporting line.

The effect of this has been to enable both partners and myself as Mayor to create space for me to function in that wider role referred to earlier. The sense that I serve as mayor of a place rather than only as the senior decision maker for a service organisation is now widely accepted.

In taking the LSP forward, I work closely with the two vice-chairs of the LSP – one from the community and one from another service provider. In recent months, the LSP has had our Local Area Agreement at the top of its agenda and it will continue to lead on taking this forward.

The most recent evaluation of the LSP highlighted the following key points:

- the excellent analysis, strong evidence and 'what works' base which informs the LSP's interventions;

- the way that all NRF activities include proposals for mainstreaming; and

- a genuinely multi-agency approach to tackling disadvantage.

It has been possible to use the mayoralty to act as a bridge between the partners and the Council because the Mayor must set out to pursue a role which goes beyond simply being the senior decision maker at the Town Hall and offer real leadership to the community as whole as well as to disparate groups and neighbourhoods within the community.

Conclusion

Executive mayors are not simply leaders with more power – there is a public expectation that is very different. We are expected to be highly visible, and to pursue a role that is quite distinct from that of the council as service provider. That we have to address service issues, plan budgets and implement major capital schemes as well provides us with capacity and weight when we set out to work with partners or offer credible leadership on a wider stage.

Put more simply, because I run an efficient refuse collection service and get the potholes filled in, I have greater credibility when I ask citizens to be tolerant of difference, report graffiti and recycle more.

5 *An integrated approach to tackling anti-social behaviour*

Mayor Robin Wales

Anti-social behaviour (ASB) is a major concern to people in Newham, as it is for people across the country. The subject resonates even with those who have no personal experience of crime. Its effects are more far reaching than the incidence of ASB itself; and it engenders a fear and insecurity, which cements social exclusion and is a barrier to economic prosperity.

In order to tackle it we need a holistic approach that integrates the actions of all public sector agencies and beyond. We need to address the needs of those who live in fear of ASB, as well as the poverty, worklessness, boredom and poor housing that create areas where ASB blights people's lives.

The above observations are hardly new. They encompass what Labour has said about crime since Tony Blair was Shadow Home Secretary. Yet they are lessons which nationally we are still struggling to implement across the whole range of public services. In Newham, having a directly elected mayor means that we deliver the integrated approach that Labour first championed and we are reaping the rewards.

The potential for elected mayors to tackle crime and anti-social behaviour has long been recognised. Peter Mandelson, writing for NLGN in 2002, argued that elected mayors could ensure that "a strategic vision and mandate to deliver solutions on social exclusion and crime can be implemented across the council and incorporated through every cabinet portfolio and council department".[7] This is undoubtedly what we've done in Newham. But our approach goes beyond the limits of those services directly administered by the Council.

Commentators on the progress of mayoral authorities have rightly highlighted the quicker pace of decision-making and firmer action on local priorities. They tend however, to focus on the way in which the mayor's manifesto gets 'rubber

---

[7] Mandelson, P. (2002) 'Tackling Crime and Social Exclusion' in Parker, I. and Randle, A. (eds) *Beyond SW1: Elected Mayors and the renewal of Civic Leadership*, London: New Local Government Network

stamped' by the electorate, thus delivering the legitimacy for the mayor to act on his or her own agenda. Mayors are in fact more than just policy makers around an agenda confined to the prior pledges in a manifesto. We were envisaged as champions of our localities and champions of residents' priorities. Mayors have a mandate, not only to fulfil manifesto commitments, but to respond in an equally robust manner to the community's demands.

This links to a further debate surrounding the mayoral model, regarding whether mayors act effectively as community leaders and mayors of their borough in the widest context, or just as more powerful leaders of the council machinery. This is an academic debate in many ways. It is clear that the residents of Newham expect me to deliver on their priorities, whether they fall within the traditional remit of the Council or not. This means that the Council must act in new and innovative ways and I must use my mandate to make sure other agencies react to local needs.

In Newham, this means I have set up an ASB service centred on residents' demands. The focus of the service is on frontline staff. Newham has fifty full-time officers working with the public to investigate and record ASB, and to enforce the law. Typically councils have worked to co-ordinate other agencies and make existing crime prevention work more effectively. In Newham we have recognised the gap that exists for people who want action on low-level, but persistent ASB.

At the forefront of the service is our ASB Unit. This consists of a number of frontline teams able to tackle the ASB that concerns people the most. We provide an extra uniformed presence, through our Community Constabulary, in our parks and on our estates. We expanded our Domestic Violence Team to help victims of homophobic or racially motivated incidents – victims who may feel less inclined to go to the police. Our street scene enforcement tackles wilful environmental degradation, for example graffiti, tipping and fly-posting, which create an atmosphere where more serious crime is likely to flourish and where people feel unsafe.

Ultimately we know that we need to reassure people that action is being taken on their concerns. We respond to every ASB call that comes into our call centre; and when an incident is underway, we can dispatch officers immediately to collect evidence for later enforcement. After we secure an ASB Order or a dispersal order, we continue contact with the community. We send officers to check that the problems are resolved, and to nip any emerging problems in the bud. We go into our communities to make them safer – we don't just sit back and wait for crime and ASB to happen. We do it this way because that's what local people tell me they want to see in the borough, and because it works.

However, our ASB service goes well beyond the confines of this unit. Across the Council, departments are responsible for policies which are part of our service and reduce ASB. The most prominent example is our investment in sports facilities building on the success of the Olympic bid. I ensured that we integrated this provision into our ASB service. I have made it an explicit aim of these programmes to cut youth nuisance and we target those groups most likely to cause trouble. Our estate based sports programme uses professional coaches to bring activities to under-19s, in the places where they already spend their time. This is one of a number of programmes which successfully target those demographic groups most likely to offend. Every young person in Newham is within easy walking distance of regular, free sports coaching. It is disproportionately those from the most disadvantaged backgrounds who are taking part.

As with any council leader, I am able to monitor the success of such programmes to ensure they are hitting the targets I expect. As a Mayor I can bring in other partners and agencies to achieve more. One example is our work with the Driver and Vehicle Licensing Agency (DVLA). A few years ago, Newham was one of the worst places in the country for abandoned and burnt out cars. That was until we brokered a deal with the DVLA which allowed Newham to become the first authority to which DVLA powers were devolved. These powers allowed us to remove untaxed vehicles immediately from our streets and slash the numbers of cars being dumped. We pioneered this model in Newham first and it is now delivering results across the country.

As Mayor I have been able to integrate people's priorities on ASB into the largest projects happening in the borough. Over the next decade massive regeneration will transform Newham, including the Olympic Games and our flagship housing programme 'Local Space'.[8] My work with developers and national government involves ensuring that local priorities are paramount. In relation to crime and ASB, I am fighting to ensure mixed development to make sure we do not recreate areas of concentrated disadvantage. I am ensuring that sustainable jobs are

---

8 For more information on Local Space see Wales, R. (2005) 'Don't knock this great opportunity to boost affordable housing', *Tribune*, 28 October

created for people here. I am fighting for neighbourhood design that facilitates safety in the community: no small alleys, good lighting and secure public space – exactly those things people mention to me every day in the borough. Only the mayoral model permits working with major partners on this scale and delivers this amount of community led input.

It is no surprise to us that the approach is proving so successful. We've slashed the number of young people appearing before youth courts for first time offences by 25%. The number of young people accused of a crime in Newham has fallen by 23%, and now we're below the London average. We've halved the difference in the crime rate in Newham compared to London, and last year witnessed a fall of 10% in total offences. Racially motivated crimes in August 2005 were less than half the figure of the previous August. These are successes achieved in a unique context: Newham is the 11th most deprived area in the UK, the most ethnically diverse and has Britain's second lowest employment rate.

The partners we work most closely with to achieve these successes are the police. We have Metropolitan Police officers seconded to our ASB Unit and we task a team of officers and Police Community Support Officers, directing them to the hotspots that local residents identify. Working closely with the police is essential. The Council obviously has only limited powers of enforcement and is unable to deal with serious crime. But we can and do facilitate the work of the police. The ASB Unit frequently uncovers serious crime behind residents' reports of less serious ASB. However, I see my responsibility as extending beyond assisting the police in their existing role. I want to see the police embody the community focus and integrated working that our ASB service provides. The mayoral model has provided a clear focus for making council services accountable to the community. Beyond the Council, I draw on my mandate to push the police to become more locally accountable.

Nationally and in London the police are moving in this direction. The Home Office's proposed reforms of the service are designed to 'embed a genuinely responsive customer service culture and make the police more accessible, visible and accountable'.[9] It also advocates 'greater involvement of communities and citizens' and describes the importance of keeping people informed about community safety to combat the fear of crime.

---

9 Home Office (2004) *Building Communities, Beating Crime*, London: Home Office

This is an approach with which I entirely agree. That's why it's an approach which has been running in Newham for some time. The advantage of having an elected mayor is that we've been able to take on this responsibility for community safety, and we are ideally placed to integrate this with the whole range of services we provide. The people of Newham have made it crystal clear to me what they want and how they want their community safety delivered. I've been in a position to implement those changes quickly and with rigour.

In mayoral boroughs there is a clear way to make public sector agencies, like the police, more accountable and that is to make them accountable to the mayor. I am already answerable to the electorate for community safety: I know I'm judged on it even though I have limited room to act. That's why Newham has seen a transformation in community safety; why the Council has taken responsibility for tackling persistent ASB; and why we tackle the causes of ASB – from bored youths to the very design of our borough. All of this could only be achieved through mayoral governance; and so much more could be achieved to make Newham safer, if the police were made accountable to the people of Newham through their Mayor.

6 *Regenerating the Borough*

Mayor Frank Branston

A recent national newspaper article on the pluses and minuses of Bedford said it was dull and sleepy. 'It even has Bed in its name', it discovered. 'It might just as well be called Zzzzford'.

One can't stop bored hacks having their bit of fun, and maybe there's even a bit of truth in it. But Bedford's anonymity does have an economic knock-on effect. A common remark is that people don't even know where Bedford is, and if you can't identify a place you are unlikely to take your business there, whether as a consumer or a provider.

The truth is that Bedford has been in gentle economic decline for a third of a century, and nobody has noticed. Because the loss has been gradual, Bedford has not qualified for the kind of assistance that would have been thrown at it if all the jobs had gone at once. To give you an idea, in the past ten years, the net inflow of jobs has been one per cent. That's not one per cent a year, but 0.1 per cent a year.

Bedford used to be a centre of light and medium engineering – all gone and with them nearly 10,000 jobs. The brick industry once employed 5,000, now down to 400 and the last brickworks will close in 2008. Texas Instruments had more than 3,000 people making microchips – gone. And these are just the headline items in a depressing list.

What has made up for it? Commuting. Bedford sends thousands of its workforce over the top to London, Milton Keynes and Luton. I'll stop there before I sink into a terminal depression.

Before I made my decision to stand for mayor, I visited the rural parishes in the borough to ask them what they thought of Bedford. "Dirty", they said, with "a dangerous feel" to it, "dark and sinister" car parks, "poor shops", "arteries clogged with mamas in their 4X4s", "40-ton lorries competing for space" in its narrow streets; a town full of "lager-fuelled youth" at night.

So naturally, given that it seemed a hopeless case, I did stand. On a platform of regeneration.

One thing I decided upon immediately was that there was no point in trying to compete head-on with Milton Keynes – a bright and shiny new town which had had billions of public money poured into it. Bedford had to have a distinctive offer, something to set it apart.

I wouldn't like it thought that Bedford has nothing going for it. One of the most beautiful urban stretches of river runs through its centre with meadows on one bank and formal gardens on the other. In fact, Bedford has a thousand acres of parks, and one of the country's best municipal golf courses. When one points out that these are of very little direct economic benefit to Bedford, it sometimes seems like telling a four year-old that Father Christmas doesn't exist

So I prepared a list of things Bedford needed:

- better roads, particularly a western bypass to take heavy traffic out of the town centre – identified as a need 70 years previously;

- a new river bridge in the town centre;

- redevelopment of the town's shopping areas and its bus station;

- development of the Castle Lane area in Bedford's historic heart which was cleared for redevelopment in 1963 and has remained a rough surface car park ever since;

- a high class development scheme on a town centre riverside site wasted as another surface car park;

- quality in all building schemes;

- an enhanced street cleansing programme, not just in the town centre but on the transit roads through the borough;

- improved off-street parking;

- more security on the street; and

- a rail/bus hub to reduce the number of commuter cars using the station.

So how have we (my cabinet and I) done against this wish list? Not bad actually.

Take the first item, the western bypass. Shortly after I was elected, with the help of our local MPs, we set up a meeting with the minister of roads who listened courteously to my case for advance funding for a road that was due to be paid for under a Section 106 Agreement by developers.[10] The only trouble was that under the current terms they were unlikely to have to deliver it for at least another 12 years. To my delight I got the advance funding, which provided work starts in the current financial year. But I have to say we are cutting it fine.

The development of Bedford's central area – including the bus station – is moving forward with a developer having been chosen. This is a scheme which has been talked about for a decade or more going back and forth between committees with nobody taking decisions.

Bedford has a recent history of poor architecture. All along I made it clear that architecture and materials had to be of a decent quality, in which I was backed by English Partnerships. But during negotiations with the chosen developer, there was an attempt to delete quality from the agreement. I was firmly opposed to this and it now looks as though we will at last have a suitable bus station and central shopping area.

There had been a few spasmodic attempts to do something about Castle Lane, which had come to nothing because nobody could agree on what could be done. I decided on an architectural competition which produced some good ideas that have been adopted by a developer specialising in difficult historic sites. This will tie in with refurbishment of Bedford Museum and the excellent Cecil Higgins art gallery to bring about a cultural quarter with live-work units, and individualist shops, some of which will be on a turnover-based rent agreement to prevent them being priced out by sky-high rents.

A developer is about to be appointed to the riverside site but there could still be a battle of wills between the desire of developers to get maximum returns and mine to have high quality building.

I met the allegation that Bedford was dirty with a programme of more frequent street cleansing and swifter action on graffiti, including getting advance permission from property-owners to clean graffiti from their property as it occurs.

Before I was elected, roads through the borough were filthy. I took the relevant officer on a tour of some of the worst areas. After one he asked, tongue in cheek (I think) if I had gone around "throwing rubbish in the laybys and ditches" to

10 Section 106 of the Town and Country Planning Act 1990 allows a Local Planning Authority to enter into a legally-binding agreement or planning obligation, with a land developer over a related issue. The obligation is sometimes termed as a 'Section 106 Agreement'. Source: www.idea-knowledge.gov.uk

make my point. They are now cleaned regularly and we also co-ordinate our clean-ups with the neighbouring Bedfordshire authorities so that through-roads are reasonably litter free.

Within a day or two of my arrival in office I was asked to write the successful case for Bedford to become one of the guinea pigs in a Business Improvement District, in which we obtained the agreement of the business community to raise a small levy to improve the business areas. This includes 'blue caps' to advise and help shoppers and visitors, more improved cleaning, and parking at a preferential rate in the run-up to Christmas.

Security and community safety was another early focus. Discussions with the police initially produced a lot of hot air, but no action. Eventually the police agreed to set up a town centre squad of six officers plus six police community support officers under a sergeant to deal with the complaint that Bedford seemed 'dangerous'. A night-time economy safety organisation called BedSafe has also co-operated with the police in reducing crime and disorderly behaviour on the streets at night.

Against the wishes of some of our finance officers and some councillors, I had the multi-storey car parks upgraded, made brighter and more secure at a cost of £2.9m – two have already received awards for safety and security.

Potentially my biggest win is the National Institute for Research into Aquatic Habitats (NIRAH) project. The aim is to build a fresh water Eden-style conservation, leisure and education scheme, but several times bigger than Eden, in one of the exhausted brickpits which disfigure the area.

I invited NIRAH's project director to Bedford and got a helicopter-owning friend of mine to buzz him around possible sites. He was immediately taken with an area of disused brickpits with communication links that he calculated would put 25 million people within a two hour drive of the site. Our problem was that we were competing with several Objective 2 sites without having their financial advantages.[11]

We organised a presentation in the House of Commons, the East of England Development Agency and the County Council put up £4m seedcorn capital and

---

[11] Objective 1 and 2 areas are considered to be in need of European and central government funds for regeneration. Bedford does not qualify.

NIRAH will now come to Bedford, assuming all other hurdles are cleared. That will mean a £350m project. It will employ about 2,000 people directly and probably another 8,000 indirectly, providing conservation as well as leisure facilities and scientific advances from research on genes and toxins obtained by non-invasive means. Eden has introduced £100m a year to the Cornish economy and I hope NIRAH will do the same for Bedfordshire.

NIRAH got its first taste of Bedford politics when their top team presented to a meeting of the full council after they had selected Bedford. The chairman of the project, former FTSE100 company chief executive Philip Graf, said: "We would not have chosen Bedford without the work put in by your Mayor and his PA". He left a pause for applause, but there was none; just a stony silence.

There have been other more routine projects and one or two failures. When I was elected, the general opinion among councillors and officers was on the lines of: 'He comes up with all these fancy ideas, but he'll learn'. I don't doubt that many, or even most, of the party politicians still hope everything will come to nothing; but I think they are beginning to realise that perhaps, just perhaps, my colleagues and I will be able to turn Bedford around. Already town centre footfall has increased substantially, partly because of specialist gourmet and flower markets that have been introduced.

Some are now on board. Others, instead of damning with faint praise, are praising with faint (and sometimes not so faint) 'damns'.

Which must mean things are moving in the right direction.

7 *Leadership, change and regeneration*

Mayor Martin Winter

I am honoured to be Doncaster's first directly elected mayor and proud that it is one of only twelve areas in the country to be pioneering the system of mayoral governance. It is a system of leadership that is making a real positive difference to Doncaster, its economy and people.

I firmly believe that the elected mayor model is working for Doncaster because it encourages accountability and it 'gets things done'. It gets things done because an elected mayor has the executive power to set policy and implement programmes quickly and decisively.

I was elected in Doncaster on a firm set of promises and beliefs, and I am regularly held accountable for the progress we are making against them. I am the man in the firing line, the buck stops with me. An elected mayor is subject to the checks and balances of a scrutiny committee, but he or she is freer to act without the red tape of council bureaucracy.

In a rapidly growing place like Doncaster the mayoral system provides the dynamism and decisiveness that business people want when investing. It helps us act quickly to seize the opportunities that present themselves. It helped work to start on a new community stadium within three years of my election, after it had been talked about in Doncaster for twenty years.

We are setting about transforming the town into a European city recognised internationally as a commercial, tourist and educational hub, a place which cares for its environment and people, and a place in which more people want to live, visit and build a future.

The change is already happening and Doncaster is buzzing. Three quarters of a billion pounds have been invested in the borough since the millennium. 636 acres of land have been taken up and more than 15,000 jobs created. In every corner of our borough, millions of pounds are being invested into high profile projects, which are generating a return of new era investment. Current business is thriving. New organisations relocate here from across the country to reap the rewards of our winning location. There has never been a more exciting time to do business in Doncaster. Developments such as the 15,000 seat community stadium and Robin Hood International Airport are changing the commercial and leisure face of Doncaster. The Frenchgate Interchange, the largest combined retail and transport project in the country opens next year. It will offer shoppers and visitors to Doncaster a mix of traditional and new shopping in one central location.

This unprecedented period of regeneration has brought about a real feeling of confidence in the borough. We even invited the Olympics here in 2012! Why not? We've already put the Athens Olympics in the shade – literally. The roof of the Olympic stadium was built right here in Doncaster. Seriously though, inviting the Olympics here in 2012 and our recent bid to officially become a city are the sign of our boldness, our confidence, our 'chutzpah'.

The leadership of an elected mayor provides clarity, accountability and focus, and it is through this system that we have wrought the greatest period of change and regeneration in Doncaster for decades.

Doncaster was once the engine room of England's industry, providing the coal to fuel our thriving heavy industry and the magnificent steam locomotives that revolutionised transport for the people. We are proud to hold the world's oldest classic horse race – the St. Leger – and have a long history of horse breeding and racing, due to our stage coaching past. Some time ago however, I realised that, despite our proud history and industrial heritage, Doncaster could no longer identify solely with the past. The St. Leger is held only one week a year. Doncaster's last coal mine, sadly, is to be mothballed soon.

Rather than dwelling on the past, I believe that Doncaster needs to be driven into the future. A future that will not only build on a historically excellent transport network and its hard working people, but one that will also look further than the borough, the region and the country for its success. A future built by throwing off our town and village outlook, where we are proud of our yesterday, but are bold about planning and building for a bright and prosperous tomorrow. A future where we can dare to be different, where we can face challenges in new and innovative ways, where the Mayor and the Council will challenge the old way of doing things, and lead in a way that becomes the envy of authorities across the country.

Our streets are cleaner, our children are doing better at school and we're recycling more. Every time I'm out and about I can feel a growing sense of pride in the community.

Doncaster's economic revival must be matched by social improvements in Doncaster and my role as an elected mayor is crucial to this. Doncaster's renaissance must benefit its people and lead to real improvements in their quality of life and prospects.

A huge part of my job is getting Doncaster's people on board and getting them to sign up to Doncaster's strong positive vision for the future. One of the earliest pieces of advice I was given was that 'you cannot lead people where they don't want to go'. I think that in Doncaster it is wise to heed this advice.

I also think it wise to take into account just how important a role Doncaster's history has played on the character and culture of its proud communities and people. Being born and brought up in Doncaster has equipped me to understand the positive psyche of many of our people, but it still hasn't been able to take away my frustration at how resistant to change a minority remain. One of my most difficult challenges as a leader is to stand up to those who continually look backwards: a small but vocal group of people whose inertia and cynicism lead them to carp and criticize, not to get involved or think positively.

We have the traditional 'hub and spoke' model here in Doncaster – a large urban centre surrounded by a number of outlying communities of various sizes. Many of these communities sprang up around the local mines. These communities were devastated by the demise of the industry in the 1980s and 1990s – leaving a fall-out of deprivation that is only now starting to clear. These tight communities tended to instill a culture of insularity and a strong tradition of resistance to change.

So what can I do to overcome these obstacles – how as a leader can I involve those who didn't put a cross by my name on the ballot paper in May? By making sure that Doncaster Council delivers. Delivering the services that people want, where they want them and how they want them. And by listening to their views and putting their needs at the heart of everything we do.

The Neighbourhood Management structure of our winning council has revolutionised the way that the authority delivers its services. Gone are the traditional directorates that worked so independently of each other, to use the jargon, in their corporate 'silos'. In their place is a system where the borough is split up into areas each managed by a team of people who provide a range of services right on people's doorsteps.

Through my Green and White paper system I can get the community's views on major issues to help me make a decision. This inclusive system has worked successfully on issues such as housing, special education and cleaner and safer streets.

So by delivering quality services in an efficient way, Doncaster Council can help foster a sense of pride in the community, overcome the challenges made by the backward looking minority and play a leading role in our future. To succeed, I need to lead a council that can react quickly, make timely decisions and include our people on our exciting journey into the future.

Doncaster needs to work together to recognise our huge potential and make sure that the investment pouring in keeps improving our borough as a place to live work and visit. I feel blessed to be involved at such a vibrant time in my home town's history.

8 *What difference are elected mayors making?*

Kiran Dhillon

As stated at the outset, this collection of essays from some of the current crop of directly elected mayors attempts to feed into the debate about the possibilities of the mayoral system.

The mayoral authorities are incredibly diverse – in terms of politics, experience, geography, personality, leadership style and context – but we can pull out some shared themes and lessons from these essays about how mayoral governance is making a difference in localities.[12]

Lessons emerging from this collection

Increased visibility and transparency

Local government is seen by many citizens as being an anonymous bureaucracy. The experience of the mayors, writing in this collection shows that mayors can bring profile and visibility to local government.

The general view held by all of the authors is that the public are more aware within the mayoral system, about who makes the decisions. Most feel that they are more visible and accessible to the citizens – whether this is expressed through receiving upwards of 150 letters to the mayoral office or being approached on the street at 2.00am on New Years Day. Mayors are much more identifiable figures – and, in Steve Bullock's case, ever-increasingly so – it would be very difficult for the leader of a council to achieve this level of recognition.

Increased scrutiny and accountability

An advantage of this increased visibility is that mayors can be held to account by the public. They know who makes the decisions, where the buck stops and who to praise or blame. Stuart Drummond states that residents in Hartlepool will come to him when they have a problem that needs solving or to raise a complaint.

A mayor is not only under greater pressure from the electorate to address weaknesses in local provision, but also its ability to judge mayoral performance

---

12 See also research undertaken previously by the Evaluating Local Governance Team at the University of Manchester (2004) *How are Mayors Measuring Up?* London: ODPM

against manifesto promises. The huge increase in Drummond's majority in his May 2005 re-election signals that the electorate in Hartlepool were able to give a verdict on his performance as Mayor. As predicted by supporters of the model, mayors are indeed more transparent and accountable than traditional council leaders.

Engaging with citizens

All of our mayoral authors place great emphasis on relations with the electorate, seeing engagement with citizens as fundamental to their role as mayor. Upon election, Drummond saw his key role was to "reconnect Hartlepool Borough Council back to the public and vice-versa". For Martin Winter this means listening and determining local priorities through Doncaster's Green or White paper system, or explaining difficult decisions when people disagree. In the case of Bullock, it means getting closer to Lewisham's residents through mayoral visits to community organisations, relations with the media and consultations with citizens.

Although public engagement is achievable in a leader/cabinet model of governance, the mayoral system offers certain advantages. Bullock observes that during his time as mayor he has reached more citizens than he ever did in five years as a leader of Lewisham Council. This success is due to the visibility of mayors and the personal style of politics. However, it is also attributable to the fact that mayors are seen in a different light to council leaders. Mayors are viewed as advocates and representatives of the community, rather than just a council representative. This is revealed in Dorothy Thornhill's statement about Watford that "what is heartening is that residents feel that there is someone in the town hall whose job it is to be on their side and who can make a difference to the issues concerning them". Likewise, Bullock positions himself as an advocate for the community at open meetings, letting the officers explain the services that citizens receive.

There is an expectation that a mayor is different – a leader of the community not just the council. Citizens feel that they have an advocate who can break down the 'them and us' barrier. This marks a shift in the relationship between local citizens and local government.

Evidence from Lewisham demonstrates that consultation and engagement has a positive impact. 69% of the borough's residents think the Council is doing a good job – a figure 5% above the London average. The ability of a mayor to engage with the public can therefore help build trust and increase satisfaction in the community.

Making local government matter

The increased visibility and accountability of mayors, together with their ability to engage the public can therefore enhance local democracy and reconnect citizens to local government. Also, and as Thornhill points out in relation to Watford, mayoral contests have marked a shift from people using local elections to express dissatisfaction with central government to being focused on local issues. This has the effect of promoting local government, making it more relevant to people.

Having a single, visible and authoritative figure also enhances the profile of local government in the local media. The advantage of the mayoral system is that there is one authoritative spokesman for the council, which makes it easier for the local media to engage with the authority. Such increased engagement not only means increased recognition of the mayor but a higher profile for local democracy in general.

Pulling local stakeholders together

All the mayors place emphasis on working closely with their local partners. Mayors seem to be experiencing a different relationship with local partners because of their electoral mandate and area-wide focus. In Lewisham, for example, the LSP opted to have the Mayor as Chair because they recognised the post-holder would have a wider remit than a council leader. In Watford, the Mayor's direct mandate from the electorate gave Thornhill moral authority when bringing together public and private partners to get agreement for a new hospital. In Newham, Robin Wales has found that his position as Mayor has allowed him to bring partners on board to tackle anti-social behaviour. And in Hartlepool, the Mayor was able to use his influence to pull together local partners to deliver 'Operation Cleansweep'.

Of course, it is possible that a council leader could command the same authority from local partners as a mayoral counterpart. However, it is worth noting that local partners and agencies have a different attitude towards mayors because of their mandate. Wales asserts that his mayoralty gives him an added legitimacy that enables him to bring in other partners and achieve more. Indeed, the experience of all of our mayoral authors suggests that there is a different relationship developing with local partners.

Representing and acting as ambassador for the whole locality

It comes across quite clearly in a number of the essays that mayors feel they are leaders of the whole area. Mayors have a unique mandate derived from their direct election across the locality, which allows them to act as mayor of the town or city rather than mayor of just the council. Wales argues that the citizens of Newham expect him to deliver on priorities, whether they fall within the traditional remit of the council or not. As Mayor, they expect him to be able to sort out all problems in the area and he is judged on services that are not part of the Council's traditional remit. While this is not necessarily unique to mayoral authorities, it is a role that the mayors have embraced and are able to act upon.

As community leaders, mayors also have a definite vision for their locality, not just council services. So Frank Branston talks about a vision for Bedford focussed not just on council services but things beyond the traditional remit of the council, such as attracting inward investment and tackling crime. Likewise in Doncaster, the Mayor has a bold and ambitious view about the future well-being of the town. Winter has a visionary outlook, seeking to transform it into a European city. By campaigning for funding and investment, and forging relationships with key stakeholders, mayors are acting as ambassadors for their areas. Their ability to play this role can deliver real improvements, as illustrated by the regeneration and economic development taking place in Doncaster and Bedford.

Integrated approach

Elected mayors' ability to pull local partners together and their role as representatives of the locality, also allows mayoral governance to support a holistic and integrated approach to public service delivery. Mayors are able to take a strategic view across the area and deliver an integrated solution to problems. This is certainly the approach taken towards anti-social behaviour in Newham. Wales has not only embedded solutions across council services but because of his influence and authority over local partners, he is able to work with other local agencies to co-ordinate an integrated response.

Service delivery and improvement

Research shows that an advantage of the mayoral system is that ultimately, decisions lie with one person. There is also benefit in having a four-year term of office. Mayors can plan a long-term strategy and make difficult decisions without worrying about reselection each year.

Many of our mayoral authors comment on difficult decisions they have taken, and which had been put off by the previous administration. In the case of Bedford, Branston very swiftly made a decision over the redevelopment of the town centre and bus station which had been talked about for a decade. He was also able to organise a helicopter tour of the town at short notice when NIRAH's project director considered Bedford a location for their conservation project. In Doncaster, within three years of Winter's election as Mayor, they are building a new community stadium that had been talked about for two decades.

Both the quicker pace of decision-making and their strategic view across their locality means mayors are having a positive impact on service delivery. Wales credits mayoral governance with helping to achieve a 10% fall in total criminal offences, halving the difference of the crime rate in Newham when compared to London. In Hartlepool, Operation Cleansweep has delivered on the liveability agenda. And in Bedford, development is underway on the regeneration of the town's shopping areas and bus station.

Mayoral governance does not therefore merely represent more visible and accountable leadership. It is also driving service improvements in localities.

Economic development and inward investment

A noticeable outcome of the mayoral system has been greater economic development and inward investment. For Drummond, the business community in Hartlepool view him as having the influence and leadership to drive the local economy. In Doncaster meanwhile, millions of pounds are being invested, businesses are relocating to the town and jobs are being created. As Winter remarks in his essay, "the mayoral system provides the dynamism and decisiveness that business people want when investing". Branston's ability to attract the NIRAH to Bedford has not only created employment opportunities in the town, but boosted its economy.

An elected mayor acts as an ambassador for their area – a representative who can articulate a vision and aspiration for the area. They are a single authoritative spokesperson to the world outside their locality. Their high visibility ensures that they are identifiable to the business community and other key stakeholders, but together with their direct election it ensures they remain accountable to the electorate. And the evidence from our essays clearly suggests that the mayoral system is capable of attracting inward investment, and that mayors have the ability to seize economic opportunities.

9 *Conclusion: where next for directly elected leadership?*

Kiran Dhillon

While it would be premature to draw absolute conclusions about the difference that mayors have made, we can extract a few areas where they are having a distinctive impact.

These essays illustrate that a figure who is directly elected can achieve a high level of visibility and accountability. As a figurehead they are also able to raise the profile of an area and provide a focal point for businesses, with the benefit of attracting inward investment. And the mayors also feel that a direct democratic mandate has given them the authority to pull partners together and deliver integrated, joined-up delivery. How then do the experiences of mayoral governance help us to think about the future of local governance?

Strong leader/directly elected cabinets

The essays have picked up on some of the unique features of mayoral governance, but it could be argued that some of the examples are achievable by a strong leader with a supportive cabinet or a directly elected cabinet. It is therefore helpful to extract the lessons from the mayoral experience and ask what they have to offer a directly elected cabinet or a strong leader and cabinet. What if any are the features of mayoral governance that can be transferred to these forms of governance? And what can be learnt about the style of leadership associated with mayoral governance?

It would be very difficult for either a strong leader and cabinet, or a directly elected cabinet to achieve the level of visibility that an elected mayor does; and the system would not be as transparent to the public. However, it might be possible for a leader and cabinet to achieve a higher level of visibility and accountability through direct elections by the whole of their area. Just as elected mayors derive their unique mandate from direct and whole area elections, so too could a cabinet. Direct area-wide elections could mean that citizens and local partners view the executive in the same light as mayors: as community leaders with a mandate and remit that goes wider than the affairs of the council. If they are directly elected by the whole area, then the cabinet may also see themselves primarily as representatives and advocates of the community, rather than simply senior decision makers at the council.

Elected mayors benefit from their four-year terms. It provides stability and allows planning and implementation over a much longer period. The Government mooted the idea of four-year terms for all councils in the local:vision paper published last January.[13] The experience of the mayors suggests that there would be advantages to giving directly elected cabinets a four-year term. Currently, a leader of a council can be changed annually via internal party group elections. This means that leaders of councils can be inward-facing, looking to secure their reselection the following year. For a directly elected cabinet, the stability of a four-year term may help them become more outward-facing, utilising their time by engaging citizens and developing relationships with local partners.

City region mayors

One option for strategic-level government being discussed at present is the notion of the city region, led possibly – although not necessarily – by a directly elected mayor.[14] Our essays suggest that such arrangements might benefit from the type of leadership that mayoral governance has to offer.

The final report of NLGN's City Regions Commission, published in December 2005, argues that city regions could not only take the strategic measures necessary to drive economic development, but also fill a democratic gap at the regional level.[15] Lifestyle patterns and identities reach beyond the local authority to encompass a wider level, and so governance at this level would represent a political form with which citizens could more readily identify.

While city regions are not appropriate for all areas and should be allowed to develop organically, where they do emerge, a common principle applicable to any such structure would be strong leadership. Just as the governance of a local authority should be strong, visible and accountable, so should the governance of a city region. In order to fulfil its objectives of driving economic development, the

---

13 ODPM (2005), op. cit.

14 See Stoker, G (2005) *What is local government for? Refocusing local governance to meet the challenges of the 21st century*, London: New Local Government Network; and, Marshall, A. and Finch, D. (2006) *City Leadership: giving city-regions the power to grow*, London: Centre for Cities

15 NLGN City Regions Commission (2005) *Seeing the Light: Next steps for City Regions*, London: New Local Government Network. Available **free** at www.nlgn.org.uk

leadership of a city region would need to be strong and effective, visible on the global stage and able to take difficult decisions and drive forward change. In order to fulfil the democratic component, the leadership would also need to be transparent and accountable.

There are various options available for city region leadership, including the executive board model, which would certainly be the least disruptive way forward. The experiences of local authority elected mayors and the Mayor of London, suggest that where local strategies have not already been designed around alternative governance models, the case could be made for having a directly elected city region mayor.

A city region should be looking to compete with other international cities. A mayor is a powerful and visible figurehead, able to act as an ambassador and bring profile to an area. They are a single and authoritative spokesperson able to represent the area on a national and international stage. As such they provide a focus for the business community, which helps attract inward investment. The ability of mayors to drive economic development has been shown by some of the authors to this collection. As Mayors they are strong leaders with clear lines of accountability, the ability to join-up delivery and who can also take quick and sometimes tough decisions. City regions could benefit from this type of leadership.

Conclusions

With the introduction of Local Area Agreements, the development of the 'Community Leadership' role, the extension of the Lyons Inquiry and the forthcoming Local Government White Paper, local government is undergoing the greatest period of change in three decades. This brings challenges which will require a different type of leadership. It is only in practice, not in theory, that the mayoral model is going to demonstrate its potential.

The experience of our mayors shows that mayoral governance offers great opportunities as a form of leadership. It can make local government more visible and accountable. It can drive public service improvement through joined-up delivery, and it is capable of promoting regeneration and economic development through relationships with business and other stakeholders. Given the pace of change in local government, it is important to learn from the mayoral model as we look to create new forms of leadership.

Available FREE at www.nlgn.org.uk

Seeing the Light? Next Steps for City Regions

The final report of NLGN's City Regions Commission

City regions are high up on the UK policy agenda, with the potential to drive economic development and enable institutions to work in ways that reflect contemporary lifestyle patterns.

NLGN established a 'City Regions Commission' to investigate further the prospects for the UK adopting such governance arrangements, particularly in England. Its final report (published in December 2005) concludes that the best way forward for city regions is through local authority confederations, developed organically and incrementally through local context and knowledge.

Mayors Mid-term: lessons from the first eighteen months of directly elected mayors

Anna Randle

The introduction of elected mayors was one of the more controversial aspects of New Labour's modernisation agenda for local government. NLGN was involved in the debate right from the start, and the lessons learnt in this seminal report (published in Spring 2004) were an early assessment of the mayoral system in practice.

Drawing on evidence from the mayoral authorities, as well as opinion polling on mayors, this seminal report reflected on the many positive signs and challenges emerging.

These publications are free to download in PDF format

Also available from NLGN

What is local government for? Refocusing local governance to meet the challenges of the 21st century

Professor Gerry Stoker

ISBN 1 903447 46 1 · £10 (1-19 copies) or £7 (20+ copies) p&p

For people in England to be convinced of the value of power being devolved to their communities, they need a local governance system that delivers something other than the 'same again' style politics that often passes them by. They need to feel confident that the local institutions they elect really do control what truly matters locally – transport and mobility, employability, crime and safety, management of the environment, healthy lifestyles, and community cohesion.

What is local government for? offers a new model of local governance in England that meets the challenges of the 21st Century. The author, a key architect of the New Localism agenda long advocated by NLGN, does so by reconsidering the purposes, functions and powers of local government, complete with new structures of governance at the strategic and neighbourhood levels. In doing so, a way forward is offered for a more accountable and engaging system of local politics.

For further information on all NLGN publications, visit www.nlgn.org.uk/publications

Copies of NLGN titles can be purchased from **Publication Sales, NLGN, 42 Southwark Street, London SE1 1UN**. Alternatively you may contact **York Publishing Services** on **T. 01904 431213, F. 01904 430868** or by email to **info@nlgn.org.uk**. Cheques should be made payable to **York Publishing Services Ltd**. Credit cards accepted.